IMAGES
of America

QUINCY
A PAST CARVED IN STONE

A sign on Adams Street designed to attract tourists , *c.* 1920. (Courtesy of Thomas Crane Library Archives.)

IMAGES
of America

QUINCY
A PAST CARVED IN STONE

Patricia Harrigan Browne

ARCADIA

First published 1996
Copyright © Patricia Harrigan Browne, 1996

ISBN 0-7524-0299-4

Published by Arcadia Publishing,
an imprint of the Chalford Publishing Corporation
One Washington Center, Dover, New Hampshire 03820
Printed in Great Britain

Cover photograph courtesy of the Thomas Crane Library Archives (see p. 9).

Fore River workers march in a parade to Boston on Armistice Day, marking the end of World War I, on November 11, 1918 (see p. 31). (Courtesy of Thomas Crane Library Archives.)

Contents

Acknowledgments

Recounting the history of a city like Quincy requires the knowledge and participation of a number of people. Around every corner I found a friendly face and an interesting story. Hobart Holly and Dr. Edward Fitzgerald at the Quincy Historical Society started me on my historical journey. Mary Clark, Linda Beeler, and Ann McLaughlin at the Thomas Crane Library secured some great images. Ruth Wainwright provided an authoritative history of Hough's Neck. Tom Galvin generously shared his collection of Quincy postcards. Henry Bosworth, publisher of the *Quincy Sun*, told some great stories and introduced me to several other people. Jim Fahey at the U.S. Naval Shipbuilding Museum could easily fill a book with fascinating maritime history. Barbara Leveroni provided the story of Howard Johnson's. Colin Schofield loaned photographs of Zildjian's. Sharron Beals, director of Beechwood on the Bay, is working to preserve the rich aviation heritage quite literally in her own backyard. Peg Cini and Mike Grossman helped tell the story of the family who founded the home improvement industry—the Grossman's. William Milhomme, Frank Sorrentino, and Mike Como provided invaluable assistance at the Massachusetts State Archives. Terry Fancher of the Quincy Chamber of Commerce, and Rosemary Fitzgerald, Quincy City Historian, always had someone else that I "really should talk to." Barclay Feather at Milton Academy found one photograph that brings a smile to everyone who sees it. Norine Lyons at General Dynamics in Falls Church, VA, assisted with some great Fore River material. Pat DeGiso at the *Patriot Ledger* provided the story of his newspaper.

Most importantly, I have to thank my family. My grandmother, Ann Merchant, told me stories of "how things used to be." My parents, John and Mary Harrigan, got me to the seminar that started this whole book. My in-laws, Miriam and Ned Browne, shared their love of local history. My sister, Mary Harrigan, watched my kids—because small children and reference rooms seldom mix. My children, Shannon and Michael John, patiently (mostly) waited while I made "just one more call." The most important person I need to thank, though, is my husband, Edward Browne. When I wasn't sure I could even do this, he got me back out there. He offered ideas, strategies, and encouragement. I could not ask for a better life partner.

Introduction

Quincy was first visited in 1621 by a small party led by Captain Myles Standish and guided by a Native American named Squanto. The area they visited, known as Moswetuset Hummock (near Quincy Shore Drive and East Squantum) is first shown on a map dated 1687 as Massachuet. In 1625, Captain Wollaston established a trading post in Quincy, then promptly departed to explore further. Thomas Morton, one of Wollaston's party left behind to tend the trading post, wasted no time in establishing Merry Mount, which, true to its name, encouraged all sorts of scandalous behavior, such as dancing around the May Pole. Soon Morton was arrested and banished to England and Governor Endicott assumed control. Quincy remained divided between Boston and Braintree, and was composed of outposts of small farms, fishing villages, and boat-building enterprises.

The Revolution did little to change the overall character of Quincy. Near the Square, the Adams and Hancock families participated in the birth of America, built houses, tended farms, and raised families. Shoe manufacturing was a major cottage industry up through the Civil War, with shoes principally sold in the South and West. Those markets closed during the Civil War, dealing a severe blow to the area's economy. But the granite industry—which started in 1826 with the Granite Railway—not only became a major industry in Quincy but ushered in the age of immigrants, who arrived to work in the quarries and cutting sheds. With the influx of jobs and money, shops opened to provide basic necessities and niceties.

In 1844, the Old Colony Railroad opened between Boston and Plymouth, making travel along the South Shore practical for the first time. In 1862, the Quincy Horse Railroad began operation with a local route from Penn's Hill to Fields Corner in Dorchester. The Fore River Shipyard had its humble beginnings in 1884 in a summer cottage on a farm owned by Thomas Watson, with money he had earned as a former assistant and stockholder in Alexander Graham Bell's fledgling enterprise. Quincy continued to grow, and in 1888 the additional services that a growing population required prompted a change to a city form of government.

The last century has seen the city grow to a current population of about 85,000. The shipyard reached its heyday during World War II, employing as many as 32,000 in 1943. After the war, the shipyard built tankers and cruise ships before reluctantly closing. The granite industry survived the switch to steel-girder construction in the 1880s by turning its attention to stone carving, and in the process produced some of the finest stonework in the world. But by the 1960s, demand had all but died out and the last of the major quarries closed. Aviation played an important role in Quincy at the turn of the century. Squantum was host to the second Aero-Meet in the country in 1910, with Wilbur Wright and a host of leading fliers in attendance. Aviation interest was so high that Dennison Airport was established in 1927. Later taken over by the government, the airstrip was abandoned and in ruins by the 1970s. All in all, a bleak picture.

But look a little closer. The abandoned airfield is now home to Marina Bay, with upscale condos and bistros. The shipyard is home to the U.S. *Salem* and the U.S. Naval Shipbuilding

Museum as well as other businesses, and there's talk that a new shipbuilding company will take up residence there too. A few granite quarries are prospering as small operations that supply custom stonework. A new influx of Asian immigrants has brought the same lively mix and vitality that their Irish, Finnish, and Italian predecessors brought a century earlier. Decades after the last trolley tracks were paved over, Quincy was connected to Boston via the MBTA. Quincy Square has seen its share of business failures, but continues to thrive as new businesses replace the old. Just try and get a parking space downtown!

When I set out to write this book, I wanted to create an "everyman's" account of the history of Quincy. I wanted to find images that would cause readers to stop and wonder if that was grandmother showing off her new bathing suit at Wollaston Beach or great-grandfather posing at the shipyard. In researching this book, I often came across varying accounts of the same historical incidents and had to make the tough decision of which version to use. I do not intend this to be the authoritative history of Quincy. Rather, approach this as a snapshot view of the city that really grew up beginning in about 1860. Take the book and stand in Quincy Square and compare the views then and now. You'll be amazed at what has—and hasn't—changed. Look at the photographs of Quincy Shore Drive. Your grandfather was probably cruising in his Model T.

Quincy is a work in progress, as are all great cities. I'm grateful that a few photographers stopped and captured a bit of what it looked like in their time. I hope you enjoy their work as much as I did in putting this book together.

Patricia Harrigan Browne
March 1996

One
Carved from Stone:
The Granite Industry

Quarry men in the "boat," ready to be lowered into Swingle Quarry after their dinner break. Quarries were deep, with straight sides. Often, the only alternative to the "boat" was a series of precariously balanced long ladders perched on narrow ledges. (Courtesy of Thomas Crane Library Archives.)

The pillared entrance to the Granite Railway incline, May 3, 1922. Notice the piles of granite and rubble high on hills. In 1924, seven granite companies were in operation, with 1,035 employees and an annual output of $3,160,324. (Courtesy of Thomas Crane Library Archives.)

Looking down the Granite Railway incline, May 3, 1922. On the right is the original granite railbed built in 1826 to transport granite for the Bunker Hill Monument as well as other goods. The railbed was so well built that for many years the upkeep was less than $10 per year. (Courtesy of Thomas Crane Library Archives.)

The Bunker Hill Monument, Breeds Hill, Charlestown. A monument association was formed in 1824 and the cornerstone was laid by General Lafayette in 1825. Plans were drawn up by Solomon Willard and work commenced in 1827 with granite from the Bunker Hill Quarry. Over the next thirteen years, work started and stopped as money ran out. Finally, a fair was held in Faneuil Hall in September 1840, and $30,000 was raised. The monument was officially dedicated on June 17, 1843. (Courtesy of Thomas Crane Library Archives.)

Air drilling after blasting at the Granite Railway Quarry. The dots are wedges ready to split the granite. Until 1800, it was common to split granite by building a fire around a large boulder and then tossing cold water on the stone to shatter it. It wasn't until around 1800 that iron wedges allowed for accurate splitting. (Courtesy of Thomas Crane Library Archives.)

Three workers examine stones after blasting at the Hitchcock Quarry. Note the ladders balanced on the ledges. (Courtesy of Thomas Crane Library Archives.)

Quarrymen coming up out of the Granite Railway Quarry in the "boat." Quarries were often 200–300 feet deep, so the only practical way of getting in and out for both men and granite was via lifts like the one shown here. (Courtesy of Thomas Crane Library Archives.)

A "four-horse" load of Quincy granite. Granite was commonly transported by railway, but horse-drawn carts and ships called granite sloops were also used to move the stone. (Courtesy of Thomas Crane Library Archives.)

The Glencoe Granite Company, 1920. Glencoe, located at Scammell Street and Glencoe Place, was incorporated in 1887 and by 1893 employed thirty-five men. Once the granite was quarried, it was brought to the cutting sheds where it was shaped, cut, and polished into the columns, monuments, and statuary that made Quincy granite in demand worldwide. (Courtesy of Thomas Crane Library Archives.)

Weighing the granite at the West Quincy Railway Station. Quincy granite, noted for its high polish, was used to build such structures as the New York Exchange, Custom Houses in New York, Providence, Portland, and San Francisco, and hundreds of other such municipal and private structures. (Courtesy of Thomas Crane Library Archives.)

In 1871, the roadbed of the Granite Railway was sold to the Old Colony and Newport Railway Company. By October of that year, the Granite Branch of the Old Colony was opened with a run from Squantum to West Quincy and East Milton. (Courtesy of Thomas Crane Library Archives.)

Locomotive and freight cars at the Berry Brothers Quarry. (Courtesy of Thomas Crane Library Archives.)

The A. Reinhalter Quarry, c. 1900. The quarries and cutting sheds attracted a large immigrant population. The first wave of Irish, Finnish, Scots, and British brought desperately needed skills—and tools—to the growing granite industry. Later, Italian immigrant workers became known for their skill in carving the stone. (Courtesy of Thomas Crane Library Archives.)

The Quincy Column Turning Company. As early as 1828, granite columns were in demand. The four Doric columns of the First Parish Church, each weighing approximately 25 tons, were cut at the Rattlesnake Quarry and hauled to the church by 37 yoke of oxen. The largest monolithic granite columns in the U.S. are the thirty-two columns at the Boston Customs House, each 32 feet high and more than 5 feet in diameter. Granite was commonly turned on a lathe for fast, efficient carving. (Courtesy of Thomas Crane Library Archives.)

A tool sharpener. The renowned hardness of Quincy granite meant that cutting tools dulled quickly. One of the most important jobs at the sheds was that of the tool sharpener. Part blacksmith and part inventor, the sharpener was often responsible for repair and improvement as well. (Courtesy of Thomas Crane Library Archives.)

Drill maintenance. As the granite blocks got larger, drilling became more important. Long bore holes were required to insert the blasting agents (first gunpowder and later dynamite). As hard as the granite was on chisels, it was even harder on the drills and bits. The quarry workers here are using a compressed-air drill-bit sharpener. (Courtesy of Thomas Crane Library Archives.)

Carving the *Titanic* memorial in John Horrigan's statue plant. Mrs. Harry Payne Whitney, an amateur sculptor, designed the statue and commissioned it to be carved in Paris. After several attempts, it was found that no firm there was able to carve it in one piece—so the contract came to Quincy. The dimensions of the statue are 12 feet 6 inches wide (from fingertip to fingertip) and 13 feet high. The figure was designed for a site at Potomac Park in Washington, D.C. The carving of the statue was done by John Horrigan from a single block of red Westerly granite furnished by the Henry C. Smalley Granite Company. Mr. Horrigan is shown here near the shoulder at work on the statue. (Courtesy of Thomas Crane Library Archives.)

The finished *Titanic* statue. The crucifix-like pose is not coincidental—Mrs. Whitney designed the statue to exemplify the sacrifice made by the men on the ship so that women and children would be saved. A smaller model of the statue can be see to the right. In the rear of the shop are statues carved for the monument work that became the staple of the Quincy granite industry by the turn of the century. (Courtesy of Thomas Crane Library Archives.)

Old Man of the Quarry. New Hampshire isn't the only state that has a famous stone face. The "Old Man of the Quarry" stone profile could be seen at the Granite Railway Quarry. (Courtesy of Thomas Crane Library Archives.)

Two
Of Wood and Steel:
The Fore River Shipyard

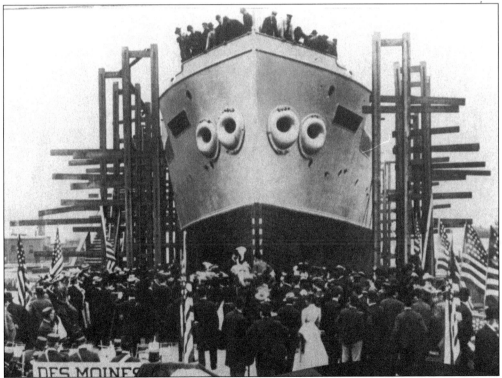

When the cruiser *Des Moines* was launched in 1902, everyone knew she wouldn't fit through the old Fore River Bridge. "The public interest in our enterprise was so great that we were sure that we could get the County to build another bridge before we could finish that ship," said Thomas Watson, founder of the Fore River Shipyard. He was right (see p. 60). (Courtesy of General Dynamics.)

Thomas Augustus Watson, the man on the other end of the line on the momentous day when Alexander Graham Bell's experimental telephone finally worked. After many exhausting years of working in the telephone business, Mr. Watson started looking for other challenges. Quite wealthy from his telephone stock, he spent a year traveling abroad. When he returned, he took up farming at his seaside home in East Braintree. The farm proved too small and the land too rocky for his agricultural experiments. He then decided to take up an old interest in marine engines. In 1884, with one employee, he founded the Fore River Engine Company. (Courtesy of General Dynamics.)

The small summerhouse where Watson and his assistant, Frank O. Wellington, first started designing and building marine engines. The first rotary steam engines proved to be a complete failure, but a second attempt at small engines designed for yachts and tug boats was such a success that Watson made Wellington a partner. (Courtesy of General Dynamics.)

Groundbreaking at the new yard, 1900. When Fore River won a contract to build the USS *Des Moines*, Watson and Wellington broke ground at the present shipyard site, located 2 miles downstream. For five years, while Watson concentrated on building ships, Wellington built the new shipyard. He even floated a four-story office building over—complete with occupants inside! (Courtesy of General Dynamics.)

A growing business. With successful bidding on navy contracts, many private commissions, and engine work, the shipyard continued expanding. This was the main entrance to the Fore River Ship and Engine Company in 1902, located at 97 East Howard Street. (Courtesy of General Dynamics.)

Fore River Ship and Engine Company, 1902. By the time this view of the company was taken, the shipyard was already earning a reputation for quality work. Four navy vessels were either contracted or under construction. The only seven-masted schooner ever built anywhere in the world, the *Thomas W. Lawson*, was also nearing completion (see p. 29). (Courtesy of General Dynamics.)

The *Lawrence*, November 7, 1900. In 1898, the battleship *Maine* was blown up in Havana. Congress immediately authorized the construction of sixteen battleships. Contracts for two of the ships, the *MacDonough* and the *Lawrence*, were awarded to Fore River. This marked the beginning of a long succession of naval contracts. (Courtesy of General Dynamics.)

The machine shop, *c.* 1900. Watson installed some of the largest equipment in the world. All the electric cables were underground in tunnels built of Quincy granite. Although this was a time of rapid expansion, there was often little or no profit. Watson was periodically forced to sell off some of his shares in the Bell Telephone Company to keep the yard afloat. (Courtesy of General Dynamics.)

The *Diamond Shoals*. While naval contracts were important to Fore River, the partners also completed other building jobs and entered the ship repair business as well. The lightship *Diamond Shoals*, launched in 1900, was the first all-steel vessel to be built on the South Shore. (Courtesy of General Dynamics.)

In 1904, five submarines were built for the Japanese navy for use in the Russo-Japanese War. The subs were built, disassembled, shipped to the West Coast, and then loaded on steamers bound for Japan. Fore River also built subs for England, Canada, and Spain, as well as eighty subs for the Electric Boat Company in the years before 1924 when the EBC did not have its own shipyard. (Courtesy of General Dynamics.)

The *Thomas W. Lawson*, 1902. John Crowlely of Boston owned the only seven-masted schooner ever built. He was so impressed with her performance that he quickly ordered another: the six-masted *William L. Douglas*, delivered in 1903. The *Lawson* was driven ashore off the Cornish coast in a gale in 1907. (Courtesy of General Dynamics.)

Possibly the *Vermont*, c. 1904. In 1904, the yard reorganized to become the Fore River Shipbuilding Company. Watson quit the business with little to show for twenty years of hard work—except for the personal pride of building one of the largest shipyards in the U.S. In 1913, the Bethlehem Shipbuilding Corporation bought the yard and renamed it the Fore River Plant. (Courtesy of Ruth Wainwright.)

A productive wager. In 1918, a $10,000 bet was placed between the Fore River Plant and Bethlehem Steel in San Francisco on which yard could build the most destroyers. It was no contest: Quincy built eighteen destroyers to San Francisco's six—and built an additional ten subs and six merchant ships during the same time. Joe Tynan, the general manager in San Francisco, pays off the bet. (Courtesy of General Dynamics.)

Fore River workers celebrate Armistice Day. When the armistice was signed on November 11, 1918, ending World War I, the Fore River workers paraded to Boston. Workers could be justifiably proud of their contribution to the war effort—they were the only shipyard in the country to have delivered torpedo boat destroyers during the actual war period. (Courtesy of Thomas Crane Library Archives.)

Fore River workers marching through Quincy on Armistice Day. During World War I, the Fore River yard and its affiliate, the Victory Plant at Squantum, turned out more destroyers for the navy than all other shipyards in the United States combined. The destroyer *Reid* was built in the world-record time of forty-one-and-a-half working days from the laying of the keel to delivery. Joseph L. Whiton, the mayor of Quincy, is in the front on the right with the flag. (Courtesy of Thomas Crane Library Archives.)

The *North Dakota*, the first turbine-driven battleship, launched in 1908. Quincy had begun working with the Curtis turbine engine several years earlier. This installation was considered an important engineering achievement—and attracted considerable attention worldwide. (Courtesy of General Dynamics.)

"Fore River to Sparrow Point MD for the US Shipping Board Emergency Fleet Corporation." The electrical department building is behind the flatcar to the right and the rigging loft to the left in the background. Notice the horses in the back—they were still used for hauling within the yard. (Courtesy of Massachusetts Military Research Center of the U.S. Naval Shipbuilding Museum.)

The contract for the battleship *Rhode Island* was awarded in 1899 along with the contract for the *New Jersey*. The ships were 15,000-ton vessels and were considered huge ships in their day. This period of expansion was a difficult one for the shipyard. (Courtesy of the Collection of Tom Galvin.)

The battleship *Vermont*, delivered in 1907, shown here next to the 75-ton crane on the pier. When the shipyard was not busy with ship construction, it turned its attention to producing printing presses, coastal defense guns, shoe machinery, and refrigeration equipment, as well as other products. (Courtesy of the Collection of Tom Galvin.)

A Fore River worker in the foundry, opening a mold after casting. One year after its purchase by Bethlehem Steel in 1913, the shipyard was envisioned as an empire capable of turning out all iron and steel products used on land and sea. (Courtesy of Massachusetts Military Research Center of the U.S. Naval Shipbuilding Museum.)

A crankshaft being turned on an engine lathe that was capable of turning and boring shafts up to 65 feet long. Machining tolerances were as demanding then as now, and very skilled hands were necessary to turn out the quality of work demanded. (Courtesy of General Dynamics.)

A Fore River engineer checks the tolerances and workmanship on a propeller. In 1906, Fore River established an apprentice program. Admission to the program was very competitive—preference was given to the sons and nephews of current workers. Workers could choose an apprenticeship from more than fifteen trades offered. Apprentices attended eight thousand hours of training over the course of four grading periods. Grades below a "C" meant another five hundred hours of training. (Courtesy of General Dynamics.)

A rivet-heating furnace. James J. Kilroy was hired to count rivet holes. When he finished a section, he would sign "Kilroy was here." Due to the large number of ships and their worldwide travel, "Kilroy" became an intriguing, popular figure. Mr. Kilroy went onto become a city councilor in Boston. (Courtesy of Massachusetts Military Research Center of the U.S. Naval Shipbuilding Museum.)

Boilers being constructed in the boiler shop. A 15-ton capacity Shaw crane hovers overhead. Note the size of the men in relation to the boilers. (Courtesy of Massachusetts Military Research Center of the U.S. Naval Shipbuilding Museum.)

A workman using one of the mixing machines. (Courtesy of Massachusetts Military Research Center of the U.S. Naval Shipbuilding Museum.)

The forge at the Fore River Shipyard. The largest of its kind in the United States, the Fore River forge turned out everything from ship parts to guns (at one point it turned out sixty 3-inch rapid-fire guns). The forge was routinely on a twenty-four-hour-a-day, six-day-a-week schedule. The railway engine on the left belonged to the New York, New Haven, and Hartford Railway company. (Courtesy of General Dynamics.)

A workman using a milling machine for surface grinding. The man's left hand (on the lever) moved the table back and forth while the right hand controlled the depth of the stock removed. (Courtesy of Massachusetts Military Research Center of the U.S. Naval Shipbuilding Museum.)

Tradesmen. If you look closely at this large group of men posing in front of the loading dock, you will notice different equipment and gear that give some hints as to their trades. In particular, look for the goggles of the welders. (Courtesy of Massachusetts Military Research Center of the U.S. Naval Shipbuilding Museum.)

The tanker SS *Virginia Sinclair*, launched on October 9, 1930. The *Sinclair* was among nineteen vessels built at the yard between 1930 and 1933. The United States ordered a total of seven of these ships. (Courtesy of Massachusetts Military Research Center of the U.S. Naval Shipbuilding Museum.)

Transportation equipment used at the yard, June 14, 1930. The operators of the equipment are, from left to right: (front row) L. Smith, J. Wilson, and W. Smith; (back row) Reg. Bouley, Ed Callahan, C. Pratt, G. Fostello, J. McCaugh, C. Hammerstrom, Mr. Commeau, H. Roche, R. Armstrong, J. Peroni, and R. Purdy. (Courtesy of Massachusetts Military Research Center of the U.S. Naval Shipbuilding Museum.)

The aircraft carrier *Lexington*, launched on October 3, 1925. The first true aircraft carrier built in the U.S. was almost not built at all. After World War I, there were limitations on naval armaments that prohibited the construction of battleships.. The navy had to get permission to redesign their proposed battleship (the *Lexington*) into an aircraft carrier. (Courtesy of General Dynamics.)

The *Lexington* takes a direct hit, Battle of Coral Seas, May 1942. After taking torpedo and bomb hits, the *Lexington* experienced massive internal explosions. You can see her crew jumping over the side as destroyers maneuvered in to rescue survivors. Quincy workers were so upset by the loss that they petitioned the navy to rename the new carrier under construction the *Lexington II*. (Courtesy of General Dynamics.)

Three
Working for a Living:
Businesses and Factories of Quincy

The soda fountain at the first Howard Johnson's, 89 Beale Street, 1925. To bring in more customers, Howard hired a retired German expert to teach him to make the very best ice cream. In the days of vanilla only, there were lines of customers for his "28 Flavors." Realizing how profitable ice cream was, Johnson rented a shack along Wollaston beach for the summer for $500—and made $30,000 in sales. (Courtesy of Franchise Associates/Howard Johnson's, Inc.)

The exterior of the first Howard Johnson's at 89 Beale Street, 1925. The week before Christmas, 1925, Howard Johnson, age twenty-seven and already in debt, bought the Walker-Barlow drug store next to the railway station in Wollaston. Signs outside the store advertised patent medicine and newspapers, but business was a struggle. (Courtesy of Franchise Associates/Howard Johnson's, Inc.)

Howard Johnson's, Chestnut Street, c. 1930. With the success of his ice cream, Howard Johnson started a restaurant at the newly built Granite Trust Bank. Just as the restaurant opened, Eugene O'Neil's play *Strange Interlude* opened across the street. Banned in Boston, the play attracted crowds who packed Howard Johnson's. (Courtesy of Franchise Associates/Howard Johnson's, Inc.)

A fleet of delivery trucks, c. 1940. Just as ice cream appeared to be the end to all worries at Beale Street, winter set in. *Strange Interlude* closed and business disappeared at Chestnut Street. But Howard always had another angle, and slowly business grew. He began franchising, and by the late 1930s, there were seventy-five Howard Johnson's restaurants in New England. (Courtesy of Franchise Associates/Howard Johnson's, Inc.)

The road to success. By 1940, auto travelers hit the road and Howard Johnson's restaurants were there. Just as Johnson's dream seemed to achieve success, however, World War II started and gas rationing took effect. Restaurants that had been packed one day were virtually empty the next. This road sign features Howard's son, the future company president. (Courtesy of Franchise Associates/Howard Johnson's, Inc.)

One of the Grossman's wagons, July 4, 1912. Louis Grossman emigrated from Podeski, Russia, in 1888. Within six months, he'd saved enough from peddling to bring his wife Hia and three children to America. He continued his peddler's route, moving his family from Bunker Hill Lane to Water Street where he opened his first business—selling bankruptcy and fire stock. (Courtesy of Grossman's Corporate Archives.)

Grossman's building at 37 Federal Avenue, 1915. In 1907, Mr. Grossman bought an old manufacturing plant at 10 Jackson Street and auctioned the equipment, making his first significant profit. His supply of building materials continued to expand, and gradually became the mainstay of the business. When additional space was needed, the Grossmans bought 37 Federal Avenue. (Courtesy of Grossman's Corporate Archives.)

The Grossman Coal Yard, 1921. (Courtesy of Thomas Crane Library Archives.)

The "Deserted City" at Coddington Point, RI. This was an abandoned World War I army site bought by the Grossmans in 1922 and opened for the salvage of lumber, heating, and plumbing. As profitable as the salvage was, it bothered the Grossmans to demolish perfectly usable buildings. Throughout the Depression, Grossman's purchased and rehabbed many industrial sites, saving many jobs in the process. (Courtesy of Grossman's Corporate Archives.)

The Pneumatic Scale Corporation, 1921. The Norfolk Downs Railway Station is in the foreground along with a coal weighing station (right) and a scale. In 1938, Pneumatic Scale created the first machines to volume produce double-walled flexible bags. Hundreds of these machines are still in use worldwide. (Courtesy of Thomas Crane Library Archives.)

Scammell Carriage and Manufacturing, Quincy Avenue. The company's original business was building carriages, but Scammell's saw the coming of the automobile. By 1920, the future was already taking over: note the Firestone truck-tires sign alongside the harness-making advertisement. By the 1950s, truck repair and truck bodies made up the bulk of Scammell's business. (Courtesy of Thomas Crane Library Archives.)

The Boston Gear Works, September 1921. Boston Gear was the largest factory in the country producing standardized gears. The Wright Brothers used Boston gears in their airplane. When the Smithsonian began the restoration of the Wrights' plane, they were able to order the exact gears that the Wrights had used right out of the current Boston Gear catalog. (Courtesy of Thomas Crane Library Archives.)

A Boston Gear excursion to Rocky Point, Rhode Island, in 1912. This outing required a jaunt of 65 miles in an open trolley car—a testament to the fortitude of the revelers and a public transportation system that, unfortunately, no longer exists on this scale. This photograph was taken at the intersection of Hancock Street and Billings Road. (Courtesy of the Collection of Tom Galvin.)

The Patriot, c. 1880. On January 7, 1837, John Adams Green and Edmund Butler Osborne started *The Quincy Patriot* at their print shop at 64 Hancock Street. Osborne left after three months, but Green continued on until his death in 1861. His widow, Elizabeth, took over the paper and ran it with George Prescott. *The Quincy Daily Ledger* started in 1890. In 1916, the *Patriot* and the *Ledger* merged to form a single newspaper. (Courtesy of Quincy Historical Society.)

The Patriot Ledger, c. 1970. By the early 1920s, the newspaper had outgrown its old headquarters. In 1924, *The Patriot Ledger* moved into a specially constructed building at 13 Temple Street. As the paper grew in size, the printing was moved first to locations near Temple Street, then down to Folsom Street, and finally to the present site at Crown Colony Drive. (Courtesy of *The Patriot Ledger.*)

Quincy Sun publisher Henry Bosworth
(far right). Bosworth was a reporter for
The Boston Traveler in 1957 when he
heard about a lonely boy named Francis
who wanted "four or six cards—funny
ones" for his birthday. Henry's story
about Francis brought 500,000 pieces of
mail. Jerry Lewis heard about Francis,
and got NBC to furnish a closed-circuit
hookup from Hollywood to Francis's
hospital, setting the stage for the first
Muscular Dystrophy Telethon.
(Courtesy of *The Quincy Sun*.)

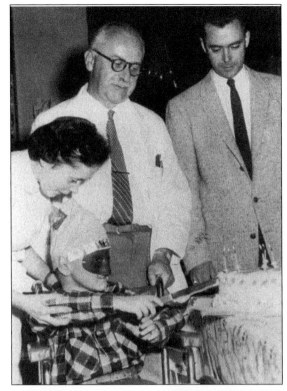

The Quincy Sun, 1975. *The Quincy Sun*
started at 7 Foster Street on September
26, 1968. A year later, the newspaper
moved to the Mutual building above
the Kincaide furniture store (since
burned down). Here, the newspaper's
sign is hoisted into place during the
move to its present location at 1372
Hancock Street in 1975. (Courtesy of
The Quincy Sun.)

Zildjian, 1929. In 1929, Aram Zildjian wrote to his nephew, Avedis III, informing him that it was his turn to take over the family cymbal business. Avedis III persuaded his uncle to come to America and set up a manufacturing facility in Quincy. Aram is seated second from the left and Avedis III is third from the left. Zildjian is Turkish for "cymbal smith." (Courtesy of Avedis Zildjian Company.)

Chick Webb, c. 1940. Zildjian has long attracted the admiration of the premier musicians in the world. Starting in the 1930s, Avedis Zildjian, and later his son Armand, worked with such musical greats as Gene Krupa, Chick Webb, Buddy Rich, and Steve Smith. Chick Webb, standing outside the Zildjian Company, is most famous for his "A-tisket, A-tasket" recording with Ella Fitzgerald. (Courtesy of Avedis Zildjian Company.)

Avedis Zildjian, c. 1935. When it was his turn to take over the family business, Avedis Zildjian sensed that the musical scene was shifting to the United States. He and his uncle, Aram, set up manufacturing in Quincy following the original Turkish layout as closely as possible. Avedis set to work under his uncle's tutelage and soon became a master cymbal smith. (Courtesy of Avedis Zildjian Company.)

Jo Jones, c. 1940. Jo Jones joined Walter Page's Blue Devils band in 1927. In 1934, he joined Count Basie and revolutionized jazz when he changed the pulse of the music from the bass drum to the hi-hat cymbal. The hi-hat was invented and perfected at Zildjian's. Whenever their tours permitted, musicians stopped in to visit Zildjian to see and try what was new. (Courtesy of Avedis Zildjian Company.)

Heffernan's Shoe Store, next to Berry Brothers. Shoe-making was a major cottage industry up through the Civil War. In 1855, over 85,000 pairs of boots and shoes were produced and sold—primarily in the South. Those markets closed during the Civil War, dealing a severe blow to the area's economy. The arrival of shoe-making machinery was even more devastating, and by 1890, the cottage industry had all but disappeared. (Courtesy of the Collection of Tom Galvin.)

Walsh's Pharmacy in South Quincy on Copeland Street near Cross Street (see p. 122). (Courtesy of Quincy Historical Society.)

Four

Getting Around:
From Horse-drawn Buggies
to Trolleys and Automobiles

The Quincy and Boston Railway at Hancock Street north of Squantum Street. John H. Duggan is on the front platform. By the 1860s horsecars (often called "hay burners" for the number of horses required to pull the heavy cars) were a familiar sight. In 1888, Frank Sprague, a former assistant of Thomas Edison, devised an effective electric car system in Virginia. Soon, electric streetcars were everywhere. (Courtesy of Quincy Historical Society.)

A milk wagon, *c.* 1919. This old milk wagon was labeled "ancient" when this photograph was taken. (Courtesy of Thomas Crane Library Archives.)

Timberlake and Small, *c.* 1890. Long before the arrival of tractor trailers and warehouse deliveries, traveling sales wagons were the lifelines for small shops and homes scattered through Quincy and beyond. This Timberlake and Small wagon sold and delivered Sunshine Biscuits and other necessities. (Courtesy of Quincy Historical Society.)

The stagecoach, a Boston innovation of 1727. They were designed to provide transportation between Boston and the thriving, but somewhat distant, surrounding towns. At first, the coaches had little competition. But by the 1850s, tracks were being laid for the car lines that would end the era of the coach. Here, a coach is fitted out for a Fourth of July parade. (Courtesy of Quincy Historical Society.)

The Old Colony Bridge landing, September 1916. One of the biggest impediments to travel to Boston was the Neponset River. By the early 1700s, there was a regular ferry that ran near the end of Hancock Street. But it was not until 1802 that a toll bridge was erected at the end of Hancock Street. (Courtesy of the Metropolitan District Commission and the Massachusetts State Archives.)

The Old Colony Bridge, September 1916. In 1844, the Old Colony line established the first passenger service from Boston through Quincy to Plymouth. Part of their charter allowed them to build a bridge over the Neponset in 1846. The landing of the Old Colony Bridge was near the present site of the Neponset Bridge. (Courtesy of the Metropolitan District Commission and the Massachusetts State Archives.)

The Old Colony Bridge, September 1916. By the turn of the century, electric streetcars were the preferred method of transportation for most short trips. They were cheap, fast, and if you were on friendly terms with the driver, they would often deposit you right at your door. But by 1916, automobiles were starting to make inroads and the bridge was beginning to show its age. (Courtesy of the Metropolitan District Commission and the Massachusetts State Archives.)

Building the Neponset River Bridge, August 1923. One of the biggest problems with the old bridge was that is was made of wood. Sparks from passing trolley cars would often ignite fires on the dry wood. And as other traffic increased, the span was no longer adequate for the loads it supported. (Courtesy of the Metropolitan District Commission and the Massachusetts State Archives.)

The Neponset River Bridge, August 1923. The Neponset River Bridge that replaced the Old Colony Bridge was of heavier construction to handle the increased weight and frequency of travel. Notice the double arch span with the wood still in place as the masons added stones. (Courtesy of the Metropolitan District Commission and the Massachusetts State Archives.)

The Fore River Bridge, 1902. The original wooden bridge over the Fore River was an obvious obstacle to building large ships. When the Fore River yard began work on the cruiser *Des Moines*, everyone knew she wouldn't fit through the old Fore River Bridge. Thomas Watson believed the county would build a new bridge to allow the *Des Moines* passage to the sea, and he was right. In 1902, Watson won the contract to build a new swing bridge, which was floated into place on barges at high tide and lowered onto its foundation by the falling tide. The *Des Moines* was launched shortly after. (Courtesy of General Dynamics.)

The Granite Branch Bridge, 1905. Steam shovels and bulldozers were still years away when this bridge along the Furnace Brook Parkway was built in 1905. Digging was dirty, hard work done by hands and shovels. And horsecarts were the dump trucks of their day. (Courtesy of the Metropolitan District Commission and the Massachusetts State Archives.)

The Granite Branch Bridge, 1906. By April 1906, the Granite Branch Bridge was nearly completed. The Furnace Brook Parkway was constructed shortly after. (Courtesy of the Metropolitan District Commission and the Massachusetts State Archives.)

An early locomotive of the Fore River shipyard, *c*. 1905. Moving the massive ship parts or materials required a railroad within the shipyard. (Courtesy of General Dynamics.)

The 1890 Dimmock Street collision. While rail travel was generally safe, there was a railway wreck in 1890 that is particularly remembered. The Dimmock Street Bridge was the site of this collision between a freight train and a work train. This was also the location of a wreck two years later. (Courtesy of Thomas Crane Library Archives.)

The Norfolk Downs Railroad Station, *c.* 1915. The Old Colony Railway spared no expense in constructing attractive, beautiful stations for the comfort and convenience of their riders. This station was built at a cost of $10,000. The name "Norfolk Downs" came as the result of a contest held in 1892 by a land company to attract buyers. (Courtesy of Thomas Crane Library Archives.)

The Wollaston Railway Station, *c.* 1919. The Wollaston Land Company was organized in 1870 to develop 600 acres of land once owned by Anne Hutchinson. As an inducement, purchasers were given one year of free transportation on the Old Colony Railway. Howard Johnson started his empire in 1925 in the building on the right. (Courtesy of Thomas Crane Library Archives.)

Old Colony Company trolley cars, probably freight or combination cars. Early streetcars were elaborate affairs, built by cabinetmakers with fine woods, upholstered in leather and velvet, with rattan seats available for smokers. Itinerant sign painters decorated the cars lavishly with gold leaf. Fittings of brass and stained glass served to decorate as well as mark the color of the cars for illiterate persons or non-English-speaking immigrants. Businesses quickly realized that they could use the routes for deliveries, and parcels were often handed to the conductor with instructions to leave them off a few stops down the line. Streetcar companies realized that there was a market to be served and started charging for deliveries. Freight included everything from the U.S. Mail to milk. To meet the demand, freight cars were added to the runs, sometimes cleverly disguised as passenger cars so that townspeople would not get upset at seeing freight cars rolling down the middle of their streets. (Courtesy of Quincy Historical Society.)

A streetcar, Quincy Square, *c.* 1900. Once electricity proved practical, streetcars quickly became common almost everywhere. Streetcar owners could buy anything from the quintessential open-air car of memory to owner's cars complete with wicker furniture and private dining areas. Engineers were just as busy as the designers, constantly improving the power and load-carrying capacity of the cars. One side benefit of the streetcars was that it made electricity much more available. The streetcar companies built the infrastructure to generate and deliver the power. In fact, when streetcar companies laid out routes, farmers were often anxious to have the lines run through their property. After all, it provided transportation from their own back door and excess power could be bought by nearly anyone along the line. Improvements in generators also made electricity more affordable and more available. (Courtesy of Quincy Historical Society.)

A steam street roller, known as the "Baby Roller" by the Quincy Department of Public Works. (Courtesy of Thomas Crane Library Archives.)

The Atlantic Boulevard Garage, c. 1920. (Courtesy of Thomas Crane Library Archives.)

A jitney in Quincy Square, August 1919 (Courtesy of Thomas Crane Library Archives.)

A New England winter in the age of the automobile. Snow removal was still a new winter chore for the Quincy Department of Public Works in 1921. With the arrival of auto traffic, roads that previously only had to be rolled and packed down for sleigh traffic now had to be cleared for the much less robust autos. (Courtesy of Thomas Crane Library Archives.)

The Lighthouse Filling Station, September 26, 1930. The Lighthouse Filling Station on the Southern Artery still had an ocean view back in 1930. Note the open-air auto lift on the left. (Courtesy of Thomas Crane Library Archives.)

The Presidents Bridge traffic beacon, June 1922. This beacon was the latest in traffic control. (Courtesy of Thomas Crane Library Archives.)

Five

Fun and Games:
Sports, Recreation, and Festivities

A swim at the quarries. Even though beaches and ponds were readily available, skinny dipping at the Quincy quarries was an irresistible attraction on a hot summer day. These boys were students at Milton Academy. (Courtesy of Milton Academy Archives.)

International Order of Odd Fellows, Adams Building, *c.* 1891. The Odd Fellows order was first established in the U.S. in 1819. The original order was founded to help the working man. By the 1840s, the order adopted formalized initiations and built elaborate halls. The fraternal orders reached their peak around the turn of the century. (Courtesy of Thomas Crane Library Archives.)

An independence gala. Fourth of July parades took many shapes at the turn of the century. Neighborhoods often organized elaborate parades with cars, wagons, and bicycles pressed into service. Parade marchers often expressed political or social statements as part of their themes. (Courtesy of Quincy Historical Society.)

Poor Man's Auto, c. 1915. This parade marcher was obviously poking some fun at the local boom in automobiles in the first decades of this century. (Courtesy of Quincy Historical Society.)

Politics as usual. One sure way of winning over voters is a wagon-load of smiling children. It must have worked—the Montclair School was built in 1912. (Courtesy of Quincy Historical Society.)

Suffragettes on parade, *c*. 1910. Voting laws were not uniform at the turn of the century. Some districts imposed poll taxes, literacy, and property requirements. Rather than uniting with other disenfranchised groups, some women actually welcomed the restrictions, arguing that votes for women and the elimination of "undesirable" blacks and immigrants would be beneficial. (Courtesy of Quincy Historical Society.)

Boston Gear Suffragettes, *c*. 1910. As the role of women changed, they began demanding the right to vote. But the liquor and textile industries vigorously opposed enfranchising women for fear that they would support prohibition and stiffer child labor laws. In 1919, Congress finally approved the Nineteenth Amendment, which granted women the vote. (Courtesy of Quincy Historical Society.)

"Snow King," c. 1900. This twenty-four-man sled, called "Snow King," was made by John Algot Erickson. He is on the far left in this photograph. (Courtesy of Quincy Historical Society.)

The Quincy Tennis Club, September 1888. Tennis was still a new sport in 1887 when the "Lawn Tennis Club" was formed and two courts were laid out on Bigelow Street. Formally opened on September 3, 1887, the courts' first tournament was held on September 17. In 1900, new courts were constructed on Whitney Road. The club remained at this site until 1913, when it moved to Glendale Road. (Courtesy of Quincy Historical Society.)

The Flag Boat, Quincy Yacht Club, 1892. The Quincy Yacht Club was founded in 1874. The Flag Boat was captained by Commodore Shaw for this Ladies Day in 1892. (Courtesy of Quincy Historical Society.)

A Quincy Yacht Club regatta, c. 1892. Regattas and races were popular events at the Quincy Yacht Club. The very first regatta was held August 15, 1874. There were four classes of boats and a 2.5-mile two-man rowing race. By the time this photograph was taken around 1892, membership had increased to the point that the club was able to buy and build its own clubhouse and floats. (Courtesy of Quincy Historical Society.)

The Quincy Yacht Club docks, 1892. When the Quincy Yacht Club was formed, its first meetings were held at the town hall and at member's homes. By 1888, the club was ready to purchase some land and build a clubhouse. Land at Quincy Point was considered, but it could only be leased, so the decision was made to build on a lot at Hough's Neck. (Courtesy of Quincy Historical Society.)

A ship under sail, Quincy Yacht Club, 1892. In 1898, the club offered the Challenge Cup for the first time to promote small boat racing. It's now the third oldest race of its kind in the U.S. (Courtesy of Quincy Historical Society.)

President Taft at the Quincy Railway Station, c. 1910. President Taft was as fascinated with the newly invented airplanes as the rest of the country, and enjoyed attending the 1910 Aero-Meet in Squantum (see p. 78). The featured flier at the 1910 air meet, Claude Grahame-White, invited the President up for a ride. But the 300-pound Taft wisely refused. (Courtesy of Thomas Crane Library Archives.)

A pastoral scene. By the time this photograph was taken, Quincy was already well on its way to the end of its agricultural age. Open tracts of land were being sold for development and farms were disappearing one by one. This boy playing with his goat and cart would have been a familiar sight at homes all over Quincy at the turn of the century, but by the 1930s such scenes had vanished. (Courtesy of Quincy Historical Society.)

Six

Taking to the Skies:
Air Pioneers

Harriet Quimby, 1912. After seeing her first air show in 1910, Harriet Quimby became the first licensed woman pilot in the United States in 1911. Less than a year later, Harriet sailed to England with the intent of flying across the English Channel. On April 16, 1912, Quimby became the first woman to fly across the English Channel (see p. 83). (Courtesy of Quincy Historical Society.)

The trophy for the winner of the amateur speed contest, Harvard-Boston Aero-Meet, 1910. The first Eastern air meet was held at Squantum. Leading fliers, including Wilbur Wright, Glenn Curtiss, and Claude Grahame-White, thrilled onlookers including President Taft, Franklin Delano Roosevelt, Mayor "Honey Fitz" Fitzgerald, and crowds of over twenty thousand people. The mayor even accepted an invitation for an airplane ride from Grahame-White, who later won the amateur speed contest. (Courtesy of the Collection of Tom Galvin.)

A dirigible, Aero-Meet, 1910. A variety of aircraft attended the Aero-Meet, including this dirigible piloted by Cromwell Dixon. Dixon wanted to win a contest by flying the dirigible from Squantum to the State House in Boston. He arrived in Boston but mistook the dome of the Christian Science church for that of the State House, turned back, and lost the contest. (Courtesy of the Collection of Tom Galvin.)

The Harvard Cup—the first amateur prize in bomb dropping. The contest required pilots to maneuver over a model warship and drop plaster "bombs." Claude Grahame-White thoroughly impressed not only the judges with his accuracy and skill—scoring 180 points in 81 trials—but also caught the attention of military observers as well. He added this trophy to his other winnings. (Courtesy of the Collection of Tom Galvin.)

English aviator Claude Grahame-White. Grahame-White had just missed being the first pilot to fly from London to Manchester when his daring, charm, and good looks prompted organizers to offer him $50,000 to appear at the Harvard Aero-Meet. Grahame-White's piloting skills were not exaggerated—he took nearly every prize offered and collected more than $75,000 in prize and guarantee money. (Courtesy of the Collection of Tom Galvin.)

Grahame-White inspects his plane before take off, September 7, 1910. The most dangerous event at the Aero-Meet was a 33-mile race to Boston Light and back. Wright and Curtiss considered the land and sea course far too dangerous to attempt. But Grahame-White was game. (Courtesy of the Collection of Tom Galvin.)

Claude Grahame-White in the air in his Farman biplane. The back of the photograph reads "Claude Grahame-White is an English aviator who came over for the occasion and captured most of the honors. He used French machines—Farman Biplane and Blériot monoplane." (Courtesy of the Collection of Tom Galvin.)

GRAHAME-WHITE STARTING HIS ENGINE FOR A FLIGHT.

Grahame-White and his Blériot monoplane, 1910. Grahame-White brought his Farman biplane and a 50-hp Blériot (one of the fastest planes in the world) to compete in the Aero-Meet. Debutantes and society ladies lined up to pay him $500 each for a ride around the air field. (Courtesy of the Collection of Tom Galvin.)

Grahame-White over Squantum, 1910. Grahame-White turned his Aero-Meet triumph into a lucrative tour. The City of Brockton paid him $50,000 for a week-long air show that the weather shortened to a single flight. Then it was on to Washington where he landed beside the White House. Finally, Grahame-White was off to New York, where he was the toast of the town. (Courtesy of the Collection of Tom Galvin.)

Glenn Curtiss, Harvard Aero-Meet, 1910. Glenn Curtiss, at age thirty-two, built one of the finest small, light engines around. When the Wright brothers showed no interest in his engine, Curtiss came to the attention of Alexander Graham Bell. "Bell's Boys" built several experimental aircraft. On July 4, 1908, Curtiss and his "June Bug" took the *Scientific America* prize for the first public 1-kilometer flight. In August 1909, Curtiss went to France to participate in the world's fist aeronautical meet. He won the prestigious Gordon Bennett Cup at the meet for setting a speed record. (Courtesy of the Collection of Tom Galvin.)

Harriet Quimby, 1912. Harriet's love of flying began at the Belmont Park Aero-Meet in 1910. She persuaded one of the top fliers in the world, John Moisant, to give her lessons. Before she could start, John was killed in an air crash. Undaunted, she took lessons with his brother Alfred. She became the first licensed woman pilot in the U.S., and a member of the Moisant Air Exhibition Team. (Courtesy of Quincy Historical Society.)

Harriet Quimby in her famous purple satin flight suit, 1912. On April 16, 1912, she was the first woman to fly the English Channel. Triumphant, she entered the 1912 Harvard Aero-Meet. On July 1st, on a routine flight in her new Blériot with passenger William Willard, five thousand spectators watched as Harriet's plane suddenly pitched forward into a nose dive. William was thrown from the plane, and moments later Harriet followed. Both died on impact in the muddy flats of Squantum. Examination of the plane wreckage yeilded few clues as to the cause of the accident, but experts speculate that Willard might have leaned forward to tell Quimby something, and by doing so threw the plane off balance. (Courtesy of Quincy Historical Society.)

Dennison Airport, *c.* 1940. On September 3, 1927, William Bradford and Harold Dennison opened the airport near the site of the Aero-Meets. Among the very first passengers was Amelia Earhart. Ms. Earhart, a social worker at the Dennison House in Boston, was already an aviation record-holder and later owned part of the airport. (Courtesy of the Collection of Beechwood on the Bay.)

Dennison Airport, February 1940. Through 1940, Dennison was the site of air shows as well as student and passenger flights. "Old Home Week," in 1930, recreated some of the events of the original Aero-Meet, including the race to Boston Light. The same flight that had taken nearly forty minutes in 1910 now took just eight-and-a-half minutes. (Courtesy of the Collection of Beechwood on the Bay.)

The Goodyear blimp, 1938. Everyone visited Dennison—even the Goodyear blimp. In 1941, the Dennison Airport ceased operation when the navy appropriated the land for an air base. (Courtesy of the Collection of Beechwood on the Bay.)

An aerial survey, c. 1935, from a Farman airplane. In 1917, the navy started the U.S. Naval Air Station at Squantum, which became the major training site for navy fliers through World War II. In 1923, a few World War I veteran fliers enlisted the aid of scientist and explorer Admiral Richard Byrd to establish the Naval Reserve Station. (Courtesy of the Collection of Beechwood on the Bay.)

A c. 1940 plane crash. The runways at Dennison were notoriously short. During the very first landing at the airport, pilot Alan Bourden was forced to land in the marsh, nearly crashing into the dike near the road. The plane shown here must have missed the runway and crashed in marsh outside airport (Courtesy of the Collection of Beechwood on the Bay.)

A seaplane, c. 1933. This seaplane landed near Moswetuset Hummock around 1933. It attracted quite a crowd of curious onlookers, including Joe Rogers (to the far right) and his friend, Tom Magee (to the far left). (Courtesy of the Collection of Beechwood on the Bay.)

Seven

Hot Times in
Hough's Neck

Hough's Neck Public Square, c. 1900. At the end of the street was the newly opened Norteman's Pavilion and the Quincy Yacht Club. The store in the center with the striped awning is Dunham's store. A map of Hough's Neck from 1856 shows only five houses on the entire peninsula. (Courtesy of Ruth Wainwright.)

Harvey's Boat Landing, Harvey's Lane, *c.* 1889. Fishing was an attraction of Hough's Neck almost from the start, and in the late nineteenth century docks, boat liveries, and boat rental shops sprang up everywhere to serve the growing tourist trade. This is where Harvey's Salt Water Fishing Club originated in 1954. (Courtesy of Ruth Wainwright.)

The Great Hill Observatory, *c.* 1905. One of many amusements available at Hough's Neck was the Great Hill Observatory, built in 1901. The six-sided structure had a telescope at the top, operated by George Odiom. There was a concession stand at the base that sold penny candy and refreshments. Admission to the top of the tower was 5¢. (Courtesy of Thomas Crane Library Archives.)

A panorama of Hough's Neck, *c.* 1895. Hough's Neck was one of the premiere resorts in the United States, attracting celebrities likes Jenny Lind, the Flora Dora girls, and the Aïda Opera Company. The Hotel Pandora is the large building in the center at the bottom, next to the pond. (Courtesy of Ruth Wainwright.)

The Hotel Pandora, *c.* 1897. When Mr. Meyer built the Hotel Pandora, he created a pond by opening a tidal gate. A bandstand was built on a small island in the center of the pond, with a clam house at the far end. In 1898, the Pandora was called the Hotel Fensmere, and still later, the Crystal Hotel. The Great Hill School was later built on the site. (Courtesy of Ruth Wainwright.)

The dance Hall near the Hotel Fensmere, November 1900. Notice the "Genuine Rhode Island Clambake" sign along the edge of the porch. (Courtesy of Ruth Wainwright.)

Sea Street, looking west, Hough's Neck, c. 1905. The large building about halfway up the street on the right was a motion picture theater. (Courtesy of Ruth Wainwright.)

Sea Street and Bayview Avenue, c. 1897. From left to right are: Cook's Photo Studio, G.W. Peterson Grocers, and Taylor's Ballroom and Bowling Alley. Cook's Photo later became the Palm Theatre before finally being torn down to make parking for Louis' Cafe. G.W. Peterson's later became Tessier's Drug Store, and after that, Kateon's Variety. Taylor's later became a skating rink. (Courtesy of Ruth Wainwright.)

Sea Street, c. 1897. The Hotel Pandora dance hall is in the middle with the long white awning. G.W. Peterson Grocers is on the left with the striped awning. Brown's Summer Ballroom (formerly Taylor's Ballroom and Bowling Alley) is in between. On the far right is Dunham's Store. (Courtesy of Ruth Wainwright.)

Electric car terminus, *c.* 1905. Dunham's Store (with the striped awning) opened in 1901. As one of the only businesses open during the winter, it functioned as a post office for about forty postal-box holders. Arthur Turner's Shooting Gallery and Popcorn Stand was to the left. At the end of the street was Norteman's and the Quincy Yacht Club. (Courtesy of the Collection of Tom Galvin.)

Norteman's Pavilion, *c.* 1910. The Norteman family opened a restaurant in 1895 on the site of the Great Hill House. They specialized in the abundant seafood available in Hough's Neck. As Hough's Neck grew, so did the restaurant. When the Quincy Yacht Club expanded in 1910, they built covered stairs that led to Norteman's so that the restaurant could serve "shore dinners" to yacht club members. (Courtesy of Ruth Wainwright.)

The Quincy Yacht Club landing at Hough's Neck, *c.* 1910. When the yacht club was first organized in 1874, there were sixty-nine members and thirty-seven yachts. (Courtesy of Ruth Wainwright.)

The Quincy Yacht Club, *c.* 1905. In 1888, the yacht club bought a waterfront lot next to Mear's pier. A clubhouse and floats were designed by Edwin Lewis and built by George Crane at a cost of about $1,800. On August 20, 1888, the clubhouse was opened. In 1910, a two-story addition was added that included a stairway that led to Norteman's. (see p. 92.) (Courtesy of Ruth Wainwright.)

Sea Street looking south, *c.* 1910. The location of this casino is hard to pinpoint, but it is thought to have been near Finlay's Store and Louis' Cafe. (Courtesy of the Collection of Tom Galvin.)

The steamer landing, *c.* 1905. This wharf was built in 1901 for the steamers that ran daily from Boston. Fare wars were common, with tickets priced between 10¢ and 25¢. The days of the steamers were numbered, however. Street car service was 10¢, available from anywhere, and did not battle the tides that often mired the steamers before they left the river. (Courtesy of the Collection of Tom Galvin.)

Sea Street, *c*. 1910. This was the end of the car line. Norteman's Pavilion was at the end of the street. On the right is the Sea Street Dream, which offered 10¢ seats for popular motion pictures. By this time, the Quincy Yacht Club had added a second story. The Boston Candy Company, next to Dunham's, is on the left. (Courtesy of the Collection of Tom Galvin.)

The Sea Street Theatre, *c*. 1905. For 10¢, patrons could see "Illustrated Songs and Moving Pictures." The most famous silent picture in 1903 was *The Great Train Robbery*, about Butch Cassidy and the Hole in the Wall Gang, who were still robbing trains out West. The film often sent audiences screaming when the villain shot his gun directly at the camera. (Courtesy of Ruth Wainwright.)

Brown's Summer Ballroom, c. 1900. Formerly called Taylor's, Brown's was famous as a center for fun in Hough's Neck. A bowling alley was located in the basement. Later sold, it finally became DiMarzio's Skating Rink. (Courtesy of Quincy Historical Society.)

Midland House, Sea Street, and Bell Street. Year-round living on Hough's Neck was difficult. Generally, the only sources of income were farming, hunting, and fishing, so the money that summer visitors spent was not only welcome but often very needed. (Courtesy of Ruth Wainwright.)

Bathing Scene, Houghs Neck, Mass.

A bathing scene, c. 1900. Hough's Neck was considered the best resort near Boston. Doctors recommended stays for "rest cures." Visitors leased small plots of land and pitched tents for the summer. Although other amusements would be available as the resort gained popularity, the natural beauty of Hough's Neck and the beaches were what made visitors return. (Courtesy of Ruth Wainwright.)

The bathing beach near the Public Landing and the Quincy Yacht Club, c. 1915. (Courtesy of Ruth Wainwright.)

The SS *Comet*. The *Comet* was one of the 60-foot steamers that made several trips daily from the Northern Avenue pier in Boston. Three companies competed for passengers and fare wars were common. The steamers also traveled to Nantasket. (Courtesy of Ruth Wainwright.)

The Hough's Neck steamboat landing, *c.* 1910. When the steamers arrived, they deposited passengers near the Quincy Yacht Club. From there, it was a short walk to shops; amusements such as flying horses, skating rinks, and bowling alleys; all manner of refreshments; and streetcars, to travel to hotels and guest houses. (Courtesy of Quincy Historical Society.)

Hough's Neck and Manet Beach trolleys, 1893. "The boys" are at their cars: Al Billings, Arthur Dunham, Merton Dunham, Sam Grier, John Baker, and Sam Williams. (Courtesy of Quincy Historical Society.)

The bathing beach south from the steamboat landing, c. 1910. (Courtesy of Ruth Wainwright.)

A panoramic view of Hough's Neck, c. 1900. The Fensmere Hotel (formerly Hotel Pandora) is the large building at the bottom center bottom next to the pond. (Courtesy of Ruth Wainwright.)

An aerial view of Hough's Neck, looking west, 1950. The road looping around is Sea Street, Sea Avenue, and Mears Avenue. The roller skating rink is the long white building in the center near the top. To the right of the rink is the old carousel at Pandora Park. The carousel was started by Dominic DeAngelis, who came to the U.S. in 1904. He fulfilled his lifelong dream when he opened the carousel in 1940. (Courtesy of Ruth Wainwright.)

Eight

Saturday Afternoons
at the Beach

Wollaston Beach, September 1916. This group of bathers reclining on the beach shows how much women's bathing fashions had changed over just a few years, from the modest blouse and bloomer costume to racy tank suits and transparent stockings. The men's suits, too, show how society was changing its view of what was deemed proper. (Courtesy of the Metropolitan District Commission and the Massachusetts State Archives.)

Along Quincy Shore Drive, July 2, 1916. Cruising the beach was a popular activity—for those lucky enough to have cars. Notice the ramps built from the houses on the left to the street. When Quincy Shore Drive was built, vast amounts of sand and rock were hauled into place to raise the road. (Courtesy of the Metropolitan District Commission and the Massachusetts State Archives.)

Wollaston Beach, July 2, 1916. Boats could be rented locally and paddling around the bay and rivers was a popular summer diversion. After a day at the beach, an evening at the moving pictures might be in order. Perhaps D.W. Griffith's *Civilization* or a Charlie Chaplin feature would fit the bill. (Courtesy of the Metropolitan District Commission and the Massachusetts State Archives.)

Wollaston Beach, July 16, 1916. The Wollaston Yacht Club and the Squantum Yacht Club can be seen in the background along the shore. (Courtesy of the Metropolitan District Commission and the Massachusetts State Archives.)

Wollaston Beach, August 5, 1917. Outwardly, things hadn't changed much since 1916, but at that moment, General John Pershing was marshaling soldiers in France for America's entry into World War I. Perhaps the gent in the suit has just come off a shift at the Victory Plant in nearby Squantum. (Courtesy of the Metropolitan District Commission and the Massachusetts State Archives.)

Bathers at the Neponset River Reservation near Dana Avenue on August 20, 1935. The Depression was on, but Roosevelt's New Deal was starting to have some effect. Picnics were especially popular during the 1930s as a form of cheap entertainment. Cookbooks were filled with advice and recipes from the simple to the sublime. (Courtesy of the Metropolitan District Commission and the Massachusetts State Archives.)

The seawall along Quincy Shore Drive, c. 1930. (Courtesy of the Metropolitan District Commission and the Massachusetts State Archives.)

Dorchester Street in Squantum. The street name is derived from the fact that Squantum was once part of Dorchester. (Courtesy of Quincy Historical Society.)

The Germantown shore, 1915. Germantown was the site of the very first organized manufacturing facility in the U.S. In 1750, German laborers were imported to manufacture glass, pottery, chocolate, and many other products. The timing was bad, however: pre-Revolutionary War restrictions and a destructive fire prevented much manufacture beyond glass, which proved to be coarse and inferior. (Courtesy of Thomas Crane Library Archives.)

Bathers at Wollaston Beach, 1924. The twenties were a relatively carefree time. Jazz and mahjong were in style and everyone was listening to the radio. The Olympics were held in Paris, and Douglas Fairbanks was amazing everyone with *The Thief of Baghdad* and his magic flying carpet. (Courtesy of Quincy Historical Society.)

The Squantum Yacht Clubhouse, 1921. The yacht club was founded in 1890 by sailors from Wollaston, Squantum, and North Quincy. It adopted the name "Squantum Yacht Club" in 1892. (Courtesy of Thomas Crane Library Archives.)

Nine

To Protect and Serve:
Police and Fire Departments

The first Quincy Police Force, 1893. From left to right are: (front row) Charles Nichol, Mark Hanson, Chief George Langley, and Joseph Hayden; (back row) John Halloran, Michael Canavan, Daniel McKay, Thomas Ferguson, and Charles Crooker. In 1856, the Quincy Police began with one constable and two cells in the basement of town hall. (Courtesy of Thomas Crane Library Archives.)

Ex-Fire Chief J.W. Hall and district chiefs, 1907. (Courtesy of Thomas Crane Library Archives.)

The first patrol wagon and horse "Old Harry," c. 1908. This police wagon was built for the department in 1902 by Henry Emerson at his workshop at the corner of Hancock and Cottage Streets. The seats could fold down to convert the vehicle into an ambulance. "Harry," renowned for his strength and speed, became the unofficial mascot of the department. (Courtesy of Thomas Crane Library Archives.)

"Sunny Jim" Murray, walking the beat around Quincy Square, *c.* 1895. In 1856 the first constable was hired. As the population increased, crime increased—and the constables often found out about crimes only after the fact. It wasn't until 1892 that a true, twenty-four-hour police patrol was instituted, along with signals and alarms that allowed officers to report in and call for help. (Courtesy of Thomas Crane Library Archives.)

The Granite Engine Company, Niagara Engine, c. 1865. In 1843, a major fire destroyed many buildings downtown. Citizens demanded the formation of a fire department. In 1844, Charles Tirrell was appointed chief engineer and five engines were purchased: two from the Niagara Engine Company and three new engines from Boston. (Courtesy of Thomas Crane Library Archives.)

The Ward 4 Fire Station, May 14, 1919. As the city grew in size, fire companies were formed at various sites to provide faster response. The Willard School is the large building in the background. (Courtesy of Thomas Crane Library Archives.)

The J.W. Hall Hook and Ladder, c. 1915, Canal Street. When this hook and ladder was purchased in 1882, it was named for the chief engineer, J.W. Hall. Originally, it was designed to be hauled by hand by a crew of firefighters, but after one or two trial runs, they wisely decided to switch to a team of horses. (Courtesy of Thomas Crane Library Archives.)

The White Company pump, Ward 6, Engine #2, 1919. During this period, the fire department was trying to modernize old horse and hand-drawn equipment by mounting it on tractors. But the tractors proved unwieldy and difficult to maneuver through city streets, and new equipment slowly replaced the old—one piece at a time. (Courtesy of Thomas Crane Library Archives.)

A pumper on parade in 1911. This may be one of the original Niagara Company pumpers purchased in 1844. (Courtesy of Thomas Crane Library Archives.)

Fire apparatus being readied for a parade, 1911. (Courtesy of Thomas Crane Library Archives.)

Ten

Quincy Square

A "Welcome Home" flag, Quincy Square, 1919. World War I had ended only a few months before, and the victorious troops were returning to America. Although America's entry into what was considered a "European War" was hotly debated, two million American men went to serve in Europe. (Courtesy of Thomas Crane Library Archives.)

Hancock Street and the Adams Building (left), *c*. 1915. In 1915 Thomas Watson, retired from shipbuilding since 1904, traveled to San Francisco to answer the phone when Alexander Graham Bell made the very first transcontinental phone call. That same year, Ford produced his one millionth car. On a single summer day, nearly four thousand cars passed by the Adams Building. (Courtesy of Ruth Wainwright.)

The Adams Building, Quincy Square, 1919. Parking was now becoming an issue. In 1925, after years of debate and no action, the Grossmans paid $20,000 for land parallel to Hancock between Clivden and Hancock Court and turned it into a free public parking lot. By 1946, the lot was worth nearly $500,000. (Courtesy of Thomas Crane Library Archives.)

Quincy City Hall, September 1919. Jack Dempsey was the boxing champion but you couldn't raise a beer to salute his victory—prohibition had begun. The influenza epidemic was claiming lives worldwide. Eastern Nazarene College moved to Quincy. (Courtesy of Thomas Crane Library Archives.)

Hancock Street, August 1919. This view is of the west side of Hancock Street from the Music Hall north to Granite Avenue. (Courtesy of Thomas Crane Library Archives.)

The Nelson Block, 1434–46 Hancock Street, 1921. Hood's Creamery and the grocers have given way to other small businesses like beauty parlors, photo stores, and restaurants. (Courtesy of Thomas Crane Library Archives.)

The town pump, Quincy Square. From 1625 to 1884, the only water available in Quincy was from domestic wells or brooks. In 1883, The Quincy Water Company was formed, and it immediately had two wells dug and a pumping station erected on Penn Street. Quincy joined the Metropolitan District Commission in 1899 and now gets its water from the Quabbin Reservoir. (Courtesy of Thomas Crane Library Archives.)

The view from Adams Temple, looking south, c. 1875. This is an early view of Quincy Square. The buildings along the left would eventually make way for the Adams Building, and large blocks of brick and stone buildings would replace the small wood-frame buildings on the right. Quincy Square was beginning the transition from small town to city. (Courtesy of Thomas Crane Library Archives.)

The view from Adams Temple, facing south, c. 1900. Compare this view with the one on the previous page. Since 1915, two churches, twenty-eight houses, fifteen stores, the Tiger Fire Company, a Grand Army building, a carriage factory, a blacksmith shop, a livery stable, and an undertaker have been razed to make way for new construction in Quincy Square. Despite these many changes, the essential elements of Quincy Square in 1915 remain. (Courtesy of Thomas Crane Library Archives.)

Eleven
Around Town

Sachem Brook, August 1905. The shack on the right was replaced sometime during the 1910s or 1920s with Elsie's, a great place for food, beer, and canoe rentals. The canoes were kept right underneath in a canoe house. The white house on the left was torn down and replaced around the same time with "The Coliseum," which, at various times, was used for auto shows, roller skating, bowling, and civic events. Sachem Brook was later covered and Ocean Cove Condominiums were built at the site. (Courtesy of the Metropolitan District Commission and the Massachusetts State Archives.)

The Adams' family houses, *c*. 1890. Franklin Street is the only street in the United States to provide homes for father and son presidents. John Adams, the second president (1797–1801), was born at 131 Franklin Street (on the right). John Quincy Adams, the sixth president (1825–1829), was born at 141 Franklin Street (on the left). (Courtesy of Quincy Historical Society.)

The Adams' Mansion, Adams Street, *c*. 1940. The years from 1776 to 1784 were difficult ones for John and Abigail Adams. The couple was often separated for years at a time, and Abigail was forced to run the farm alone. When the war was over, John was appointed ambassador to England. Abigail accompanied him abroad. Upon the couple's return in 1787, they bought the Vassall House, which they called "Peacefield." (Courtesy of Ruth Wainwright.)

View from Warren Avenue looking northeast, 1870. The tracks for the Old Colony Railway ran just beyond the row of houses in the distance. (Courtesy of Thomas Crane Library Archives.)

Black's Creek. Through the 1950s, Black's Creek was a center for boating. Sailing and boating lessons were offered on a seventeen-boat fleet. In addition to this, seamanship, knot-tying, and rowing were also taught. The end of the season was capped with the All-City Midget and Junior Sailing Championship. (Courtesy of the Metropolitan District Commission and the Massachusetts State Archives.)

Copeland Street near Cross Street, 1919. Walsh's Pharmacy is the building with the Coca-Cola sign. Like many drug stores of the day, Walsh's had an elaborate soda fountain. (see p. 52) (Courtesy of Thomas Crane Library Archives.)

The store of Mrs. Annie Jones, Quincy Avenue near Hayward's Creek, February 1928. Hayward's Creek at Quincy Avenue became the southern boundary between Quincy and Braintree in 1856. Quincy Avenue was called "The Turnpike" in those days—and considered one of the major thoroughfares running from north to south. (Courtesy of Massachusetts State Archives.)

The Casey Building, Brewer's Corner, 1919. The Casey Building was built in 1896 and housed the Fletcher Pharmacy at One Copeland Street. (Courtesy of Thomas Crane Library Archives.)

Brewers Corner, 1919. Looking down the street, you can see Fletcher Pharmacy on the right. (Courtesy of Thomas Crane Library Archives.)

East Howard Street, looking east from Winter Street, 1919. This group of small businesses on East Howard Street catered not only to neighborhood families but also to the their next-door neighbor—the Fore River Shipyard. Look carefully at the second storefront from the left and you will see that they paid "Spot Cash for Liberty Bonds." (Courtesy of Thomas Crane Library Archives.)

Newport Avenue, northerly from Beale Street, 1919. Across the street and down to the right, Howard Johnson bought the Walker-Barlow drug store at 89 Beale Street in 1925 and created the very first Howard Johnson's. (Courtesy of Thomas Crane Library Archives.)

Squantum, *c*. 1935. This aerial view was taken by a plane flown out of Dennison Airport. From 1929 through the 1970s, building and repairing yachts was one of the major industries in Squantum. (Courtesy of the Collection of Beechwood on the Bay.)

Dutchland Farms, Southern Artery, August 4, 1931. By the 1930s, the Southern Artery was the major north-south route south of Boston. Restaurants along the route offered sandwiches, hamburgers, hot dogs, and ice cream, and were the forerunners of today's fast food restaurants. (Courtesy of Thomas Crane Library Archives.)

Morey Pearl's, Southern Artery, June 1932. Morey Pearl's started in an old gas station in 1928 with a restaurant and dance halls he called "tents." His theme song, which was always in the juke box, was "The Sheik of Araby." Morey Pearl's was famous for its 157 combinations of pizza. The restaurant was demolished in 1986. (Courtesy of Thomas Crane Library Archives.)

The United Diner, Hancock Street, March 7, 1932. Diners were a favorite place to visit in Quincy—most were known for their good food and low prices. If you look carefully just at the right side of the diner, you will see a square brick building with a chimney. That is the back of the Wollaston Theater. The theater was home to "Al Luttrenger's Players" for a time during the 1930s. Luttrenger directed the plays,which starred his wife, Ann Kingsley. A different play was produced about every week, including such plays as *Ghost Train, Mrs. Wiggs of the Cabbage Patch*, and *Ten Little Indians*. Quincy resident Joe Rogers remembers that the stage door used to be open in the summer, and one day, at the age of ten, he sneaked in to take a look. The stage hands took a liking to him and paid him to run errands. They also got him in to see all the plays for free. The diner is long gone. A Friendly's Restaurant and parking lot sit on the site now. (Courtesy of Thomas Crane Library Archives.)

The Canal and Town River, c. 1930. In 1825, the Quincy Canal Corporation was formed to build a canal for the large sloops that carried granite and supplies. The Canal started at Town River and ended near the junction of Washington and Canal Streets. With the long sweeping marshes and gently rolling, wooded hills, it is easy to see why the very first explorers wrote so eloquently on the beauty of Quincy. If they returned today, they would be surprised to see the changes, but they would also see much still familiar in the natural beauty that was, and is, Quincy. (Courtesy of Massachusetts State Archives.)